THERE ARE NO ORDINARY CATS
© 2005 Rachael Hale Photography Ltd.
All rights reserved. Rachael Hale is a registered trademark of
Rachael Hale Photography Limited.
www.rachaelhale.com

Edited by J. Rose Barber
Photography courtesy of RACHAEL HALE PHOTOGRAPHY LTD.
Design by WPL

Printed in China
Published by WPL 2005

ISBN 1-904264-27-1

WPL
The Perfume Factory
140 Wales Farm Road
London W3 6UG
Tel: +44 (0) 208 993 7268
Fax: +44 (0) 208 993 8041
email: info@wpl.eu.com
www.wpl.eu.com

The smallest feline
is a masterpiece.

[LEONARDO DA VINCI]

Women and cats will do as they please

and men and dogs should relax

and get used to the idea.

[ROBERT A. HEINLEIN]

Time spent with cats is never wasted.

[COLETTE]

I can say with sincerity that I like cats.
A cat is an animal which has more
human feeling than almost any other.

[EMILY BRONTË]

You cannot help but smile
in the company of **kittens**.

[MADELAINE BAMFORD]

To err is human,

to purr is feline.

[AUTHOR UNKNOWN]

There's no need for a piece of sculpture

in a home that has a cat.

[WESLEY BATES]

Cats are connoisseurs of comfort.

{ANON}

It's hard not to envy a cat –

they know just how to relax without

having a care in the world.

[HENRY BATES]

There can't be a better life

than a cat's –

doing what they like,

when they like,

as much as they like.

[RICARDO PHILIPS]

If you are worthy of its affection,

a cat will be your **friend**

but never your slave.

[THEOPHILE GAUTIER]

It is a great honour when

cats allow us to love them.

[CELIA PETERSON]

Everyone knows that there's

no such thing as a cat owner.

[NICHOLAS HAWORTH]

Cats are absolute individuals,

with their own ideas about everything,

including the people they own.

[JOHN DINGMAN]

Training is easy with a cat. They can have you trained in a couple of days.

[GRAHAM COOPER]

Cats don't come when they're called,

they take a message and get back to you later.

[WILFRED P. LAMPTON]

When a cat **adopts** you

there is nothing to be done about it

except to put up with it

until the wind changes.

[T. S. ELIOT]

Cats can be devious and mean –

just a couple of their many good qualities.

[ALICE DIXON]

Cats are smart – it's not easy

to pull the wool over their eyes.

[RICARDO PHILIPS]

I've met many thinkers

and many cats,

but the wisdom of cats

is infinitely superior.

[HIPPOLYTE TAINE]

A cat can sleep anywhere at any time.
There is no such thing as a cat with insomnia.

[JACQUELINE FRANCIS]

If cats could talk, they would lie to you.

[ANON]

It's hard to tell

what a cat's **thinking** –

they use the same expression

whether they have seen a mouse

or an axe-murderer.

[AUTHOR UNKNOWN]

Cats are a **mysterious** kind of folk.

There is more passing in their mind

than we are aware of.

[SIR WALTER SCOTT]

Many years ago,

cats were worshipped as gods.

Cats have never forgotten this.

[ANON]

In a cat's world

all things belong to cats.

[ENGLISH PROVERB]

As we all know,

cats now rule the world.

[ANON]

Prowling his own quiet backyard

or asleep by the fire,

he is still only a **whisker** away

from the wilds.

[JEAN BURDEN]

A cat's a cat and that's that.

[AMERICAN FOLK SAYING]